SOUL DECREES

SOUL DECREES

Katie Souza

Eleven Eleven
Enterprises

COVER DESIGN BY TAD SMITH

ISBN-13:978-0-9883152-8-0

Printed in the United States of America

THIS BOOK IS DEDICATED TO MY MOM, POLLY.

Her twenty-five year illness drove me to the feet of Jesus for answers. The fruit you find here is just a tiny portion of what I learned through the process.

Thanks, Mom. I still miss you every day.

ACKNOWLEDGMENTS

I am blessed to have many wonderful people who work very hard to help me realize the vision of Katie Souza Ministries. Among them are:

My husband, Robert, my dad, Jack Caple and my other dad Jack Oates (thanks for the bail money!) my staff, the ever-faithful EEM Partners and my thousands of Facebook Friends. Thanks to the editor and the editor's editors, the graphic designers and everyone who busted it to get this thing to print at lightning speed! I owe you pizza!

Thanks to you for reading. I hope it makes a difference in your life!

And, foremost, THANK YOU, JESUS! You knew me before I was born, you protect me and show me unbelievable mercy and patience. You are my ROCK, my STRONG TOWER, my WHEEL in the middle of a WHEEL, my NORTH STAR, my BEGINNING and END. How did I ever think I could live without you?! You are WORTHY OF ALL.......MY......... PRAISE!!!!! Bless this effort and bless everyone who holds a copy in their hand. Please work fervently and effectively in their lives, I pray. Amen.

CONTENTS

FOREWORD 11

Chapter 1:
THE WOUNDED SOUL 15

Chapter 2:
TWO SIMPLE REMEDIES FOR HEALING YOUR SOUL 23

Chapter 3:
THE GLORY AND THE LIGHT............................... 33

Chapter 4:
GRACE 43

Chapter 5:
DECREES TO HEAL THE WOUNDED SOUL............................55

Chapter 6:
DECREES TO LOOSE DUNAMIS POWER 65

Chapter 7:
DECREES THAT LOOSE GLORY AND LIGHT............................69

Chapter 8:
DECREES TO OVERCOME OFFENSES................................... 75

Chapter 9:
DECREES TO OVERCOME TRAUMA 79

Chapter 10:
DECREES TO OVERCOME THE KINGDOM OF DARKNESS........ 83

AFTERWORD 87

FOREWORD

The book you hold in your hands is small but mighty.

The principles within these pages changed my life. I believe with all my heart they will change yours, too. I offer this book with my fervent prayer that it will bring healing to your soul and enable you to begin living in daily victory.

Inside, you'll find scriptures you can read and decree daily and those scriptures will bring massive, supernatural might and miracles into your life. You will release an inflowing of healing power into your body and soul and you will begin to experience restoration of relationships, supernatural health, financial prosperity and victory in every area of your life.

From my own experience, I can tell you that the authority of God's Word will establish your victory and bring healing to every issue you face. I wrote this to give you powerful decrees that, when spoken, will establish healing in your body, your marriage, your family, your business and every part of your existence.

REDISCOVERING THE POWER OF GOD'S WORD

It is absolutely critical that God's people rediscover the amazing strength of His Word to heal our souls. Consider this:

After Jesus spent 40 days without food, He was tempted by Satan to turn stones into bread.

"But He answered and said, 'It is written, Man shall not live by bread alone, but by every word that proceedeth out of the mouth of God'" (Matthew 4:4, KJV).

The word "live" here means "vital power in itself and exerting the same upon the soul."[1] In this encounter, I believe Jesus told Satan – the adversary of our souls – that the all-powerful Word of God can bring life to the wounded soul and thus thwart the devil's plans to attack us and make us sick, diseased and disordered.

The New Testament also explains that Jesus Christ Himself is the incarnate Word. The Gospel of John says, *"In the beginning [before all time] was the Word (Christ), and the Word was with God, and the Word was God [Himself]. He was present originally with God. All things were made and came into existence through Him; and without Him was not even one thing made that has come into being"* (John 1:1-3, Amplified Bible). (I love the Amplified Bible for the way it opens up and explains the Word of God. From now on, unless other-wise noted, all scripture in this book will be taken from the Amplified Bible.)

There is nothing the Word of God can't accomplish because the Word is Christ! Here are just three, of the dozens of verses, throughout the Old and New Testaments that speak of the unparalleled might and majesty of God's Word.

- *He sends forth His word and heals them and rescues them from the pit and destruction.* Psalm 107:20

- *Your word has revived me and given me life.* Psalm 119:50b

- *By the word of the Lord were the heavens made, and all their host by the breath of His mouth.* Psalm 33:6

As you can see from these few examples, the same Word that created the entire universe can also heal us and give us life. Through this book you will experience that power of the Word of God to also save, restore, repair, and heal every area of your life including your mind, will and emotions.

James 1:21 tells us to *"receive and welcome the Word which implanted and rooted [in your hearts] contains the power to save your souls..."* The word "save" means "to save one suffering from disease, to make well, heal, restore to health."[2] The Word of God has the supernatural ability to heal our bodies as well as every wrong thought, free our will from bondage and cause us to experience healthy, God-given emotions. I filled this book with scriptural decrees because they have the power to heal your soul.

In Job it says: *"You shall also decide and decree a thing, and it shall be established for you; and the light [of God's favor] shall shine upon your ways"* (Job 22:28). When you decree healing scriptures over your soul and body, the Word will be established in your life and you will experience powerful breakthroughs.

Hebrews goes so far as to say: *"For the Word that God speaks is alive and full of power [making it active, operative, energizing, and effective]; it is sharper than any two-edged sword, penetrating to the dividing line of the breath of life (soul) and [the immortal] spirit, and of joints and marrow [of the deepest parts of our nature], exposing and sifting and analyzing and judging the very thoughts and purposes of the heart"* (Hebrews 4:12).

God's Word is so sharp it can divide soul from spirit. What does that mean for you? Many issues people deal with are coming from their souls, but most never know it — so they don't take action that could set them free. How many times have you cried out to God, "Why is this happening to me?" Well, as you decree His Word over your life, its "active" and "effective power" will slice through the confusion, get right to the wound that is deep in your soul, and heal it.

THE ADVENTURE AWAITS

God wants you to *"know the hope to which He has called you, the riches of His glorious inheritance"* (Ephesians 1:18, NIV).

Are you ready to start an incredible adventure? You have nothing to lose and much to gain.

CHAPTER ONE

THE WOUNDED SOUL

*Lord, be merciful unto me: heal my soul for I have
sinned against thee.* – Psalm 41:4 KJV

He restoreth my soul ... – Psalm 23:3 KJV

Do you ever feel like your prayers just aren't getting
through? You pray as earnestly and sincerely as you know how,
but nothing seems to change.

Do you often struggle with sickness, financial difficulty or
in your relationships with others?

Do you sometimes feel dry and empty while other believers
all around you are basking in God's blessings?

If you answered yes to any of these questions, here is
something you absolutely need to know:

Your soul is wounded.

But I have good news.

Help and healing are available.

That's exactly why I wrote this book. I want to help you
get healed so you can enjoy everything God has in store for

you. You can have a vibrant, effective prayer life. You can enjoy the abundant, prosperous life God longs for you to have. You can be right in the middle of the blessings God is pouring out, instead of standing on the sidelines feeling left out.

I've learned from my study of the Word and from experience, most believers suffer from soul wounds that keep them from living up to the full potential God has placed within them.

UNDERSTANDING THE SOUL

Where are we wounded?

Not in our bodies.

Not in our spirits.

In our souls.

Some believers make the mistake of thinking that soul and spirit are synonyms. They're not. Human beings have bodies, spirits **and** souls, with a crucial difference:

The moment you surrendered to Jesus, you were born again and the Holy Spirit came to live inside you – which means, your spirit is perfect!

Your soul, unlike your spirit, is sanctified over time as you become more like Jesus.

The Apostle Paul writes, *"And all of us, as with unveiled face, [because we] continued to behold [in the Word of God] as in a mirror the glory of the Lord, are constantly being transfigured into His very own image in ever increasing splendor and from one degree of glory to another ..."* (2 Corinthians 3:18). In this passage, Paul is not speaking about our **spirits** being progressively healed from glory to glory. Our spirits are transformed

16

and made perfect in an instant. He is referring to our **souls** being healed, step by step.

Remember, the same Apostle also urged us, *"Do not conform to the pattern of this world, but be transformed by the renewing of your mind…"* (Romans 12:2, NIV).

Your mind is part of your soul, so again, Paul isn't talking about the spirit, which is changed in an instant, but about the soul, which is our mind, will and emotions. The soul is progressively healed throughout the believer's walk with Christ.

A WOUNDED SOUL IMPACTS EVERYTHING

A wounded soul affects every single area of your life. It can:

- Cause you to think wrong thoughts.
- Impact your will, causing you to make wrong decisions.
- Cause you to feel painful, negative, hurtful emotions.

Wounds of the soul are often responsible for adultery, divorce, church splits and business failures. A wounded soul can cause cancer, viral infections and other countless debilitating diseases! My point is that the health of your soul can affect and control every part of your life.

In Romans 7:20, the Apostle Paul writes, *"Now if I do what I do not desire to do, it is no longer I doing it [it is not myself that acts],* **but the sin [principle] which dwells within me [fixed and operating in my soul]"** (EMPHASIS ADDED).

17

To put it into today's vernacular, Paul is saying, "I'm doing things I don't want to do because of the junk that's in my trunk." We can't always control our behavior because our wounded soul takes over and makes us do things we don't want to do. There's only so much you can do to control your behavior – to "suck it up" and do what God wants you to do. You need to be healed!

At this point, you may be asking, "Why would my soul be wounded?"

Two reasons:

1) Sin

The Prophet Isaiah writes, *"The Lord binds up the hurt of His people, and **heals their wound [inflicted by Him because of their sins]**"* (Isaiah 30:26, EMPHASIS ADDED).

Sin can literally wound you. And, even though you have accepted Jesus Christ as your Lord and Savior – and His blood has cleansed you of all unrighteousness and brought you into a right relationship with God – there are still wounds in your soul that need to be healed. Committing adultery wounds the soul. Alcohol and drug use wound the soul. Stealing or being dishonest wounds the soul. So does gossiping about others or being a chronic over-eater. The gravity of the sin really does not matter, in terms of the harm it can do to you. Any sin can leave a scar on your inner man.

Your soul can be wounded when other people sin against you. Someone may have accused you of something you didn't do, for example, or talked about you behind your back, stolen from you, or abused you in other ways.

Once your soul has been wounded by sin it needs literal healing! That is why the Psalmist said, *"Lord, be merciful unto me: heal my soul; for I have sinned against thee"* (Psalm 41:4, KJV).

Another thing that wounds your soul is:

2) Trauma

A tragic accident. A death in your family. The loss of a job or a financial setback. A divorce. A chronic illness. Your soul may be wounded because you were bullied when you were young or because you are a parent dealing with a rebellious child. You can even be traumatized if one of your loved ones is living through a long or difficult sickness. My family lived through many years of my mom's chronic illness — and all of us were wounded by it.

LESSONS FROM A FELLOW NAMED JOB

The Biblical character Job is a good example of someone whose soul was wounded by trauma. Do you remember all the terrible things that happened to this poor guy? Raiders killed all his servants, stole his vast herds of livestock, and all his children were killed at once when a house crashed down on them. As if all that wasn't horrible enough, Satan then attacked him, putting painful boils on his body from the top of his head to the soles of his feet.

Job was a righteous, godly man, but the trauma he experienced wounded him deeply.

How do I know? Throughout his story, Job mentions the word "soul" twenty-three times. Read through the book that bears Job's name and you'll find him saying that he is "vexed in soul," "mourning in soul," "bitter in soul," and also, "my soul is being poured out." Whenever Job expressed the excruciating pain he felt in his soul, it was in direct connection to the traumas he had suffered.

Job is not alone in his suffering! Everyone on this planet has lived through some type of trauma, which means we are all wounded to some extent. When your soul is wounded, all kinds of trouble can come into your life. This includes physical sickness and demonic oppression.

Concerning sickness and disease, the Apostle John wrote, *"Beloved, I pray that you may prosper in every way and [that your body] may keep well, even as [I know] your soul keeps well and prospers"* (3 John 1:2).

The condition of your soul can directly affect the health of your physical body. A good example of this can be found in the account of the man at the pool of Bethesda. You'll find the story in the fifth chapter of the Gospel of John.

A multitude of sick and disabled people waited at a pool where an angel of the Lord was known to come and stir the waters. When this happened, whoever got into the water first was healed. John tells us that one man waited there thirty-eight years, hoping to be healed of his infirmity (verse 5).

Thirty-eight years! That's a long time to suffer.

Does the Bible tell us what caused the illness? Yes, it does. When we look up "infirmity" in the Greek, it says, "weakness and infirmity" of the body **and of the soul**.[3] This man was sick for thirty-eight years because he had a wound in his soul. And the Bible tells us that his wound was caused by sin.

Moved by compassion, our Lord healed the man who had waited so long for a miracle. But He also told him, "*Stop sinning or something worse may happen to you...*" (John 5:14, NIV). We can reasonably infer from this that the man was sick in his physical body, because the sins he committed were wounding his soul.

Soul wounds can make you physically sick, but they can also allow demonic spirits to afflict your physical body. The thirteenth chapter of Luke tells of the time Jesus healed a woman who was bent over by a spirit of infirmity, for eighteen years. Again, the word "infirmity" here means "weakness and infirmity" of the body **and the soul**. Like the man at the pool, this woman was also sick in her physical body because of a wound in her soul. But in her case that wound was allowing a demonic spirit to afflict her and cause her physical disease. How do I know? Because Jesus said that the woman had been bound by Satan (Luke 13:16).

LIVING THE SUPERNATURAL LIFE

Since I learned how to usher in healing to my soul, I've lived in the midst of a constant flow of supernatural miracles. Almost every single day, something miraculous happens in my life. And that's as it should be – for me, and you. God is a supernatural God and we are His children. If you belong to Jesus Christ, you should expect miracles.

It should be normal for you to pray for sick people and see them healed. It should be normal for God to bless your going out and your coming in. That's what happens when you get your soul healed!

CHAPTER TWO

TWO SIMPLE REMEDIES FOR HEALING YOUR SOUL

For the weapons of our warfare are not physical [weapons of flesh and blood], but they are mighty before God for the overthrow and destruction of strongholds.
2 Corinthians 10:4

In the previous chapter we discussed some of the issues that can cause your soul to be wounded and the difficulties that can result. A wounded soul brings problems like physical sickness, broken relationships, financial setbacks and difficulties of all kinds.

Now, we get to the good part.

You are about to learn two important remedies that can heal your soul and give you a brand-new life.

REMEDY #1:
THE BLOOD OF JESUS CHRIST

The first of these keys is the blood of Jesus Christ. His blood is one of the weapons Paul references in the scripture quoted at the top of this chapter – weapons which are *"mighty before God for the overthrow and destruction of strongholds."* The blood Jesus shed on the cross is powerful enough to wash away any sin that could evercause a wound in your soul. In the eighth chapter of Matthew, you'll find these words about Jesus:

"He fulfilled what was spoken by the prophet Isaiah, He Himself took [in order to carry away] our weaknesses and infirmities and bore away our diseases" (Matthew 8:17).

As I mentioned in the last chapter, the word "infirmities" means, **weakness of the body and soul**. In other words, Jesus died, not only for your sin and sickness to be forgiven, but for the sickness in your soul to be healed. If you have accepted Him as your Lord and Savior, you have a legal right to claim healing through His shed blood. Isaiah 53, puts it this way:

"But He was pierced for our transgressions,
He was crushed for our iniquities;
the punishment that brought us peace was on Him,
and by His wounds we are healed.
We all, like sheep, have gone astray,
each of us has turned to our own way;
and the Lord has laid on Him
the iniquity of us all" (Isaiah 53:4-6 NIV).

Sin wounds the soul, and when Jesus took our sins upon Himself, those sins literally wounded Him! The abuse, the beating and the crucifixion He endured caused His blood to be poured out for us and the result is that we are healed of our wounds by *His* wounds!

Partaking of the blood of Jesus is the first step in healing your soul. Leviticus 17:11 says, *"For the life of the flesh is in the blood: and I have given it to you upon the altar to make an atonement for your souls: for it is the blood that maketh an atonement for the soul"* (KJV). Notice this verse says the blood atones for the "soul". That's because the sin that wounded you lives in your soul man.

The first thing you need to do, to be healed of your wounds, is wash your soul in the blood. Hebrews 9:22 says, *"the law requires that nearly everything be cleansed with blood, and without the shedding of blood there is no forgiveness"* (NIV). Reading 1 John 1:7 confirms this, *"the blood of Jesus his Son cleanses us from all sin"* (ESV).

These are just two, of dozens of verses, referring to the might and effectiveness of Jesus' blood. It is so powerful that it actually washes away **every single sin** that has ever wounded your soul. It washes away sins that you committed. It washes away sins that others have committed against you. And it brings atonement for the instances where your ancestors may have sinned and caused a wound in the soul that has been passed down through generations.

Whenever you are seeking healing for your soul, the blood of Christ is the very first and most effective medicine you can apply.

But there's one more, very important step we must take to receive our complete healing. We also need to understand and receive a power called **dunamis** that is available to us through Christ's resurrection from the dead.

REMEDY #2:
THE DUNAMIS POWER OF THE RESURRECTION

I'm going to say something that may shock you. But I say it with the deepest reverence and appreciation for what Jesus Christ did for us when He gave His life on the cross.

Too many believers focus their attention entirely on the cross, and never go to the rest of the story.

The cross was the ultimate moment of sacrifice and atonement. There is no forgiveness of sin without Calvary. Even so, the ultimate moment of victory came three days later, when Jesus walked out of the tomb.

Let me repeat that, because it is so important. When Jesus died on the cross, His shed blood washed away the sins that had separated us from God and left us struggling under the Adamic curse. When Jesus rose from the dead, he gave us the power to be raised from the dead with Him in every part of our being – body, soul and spirit.

It is the cross, **plus** the empty tomb, that tells the total story of our faith—the death **and** the resurrection. The power of the resurrection radiates out from the empty tomb, giving all believers the ability to live in victory, but most of us are not aware. Jesus told Peter that the gates of hell would not be able to withstand the church's advance. The Amplified Bible puts it this way:

> *"And I tell you, you are Peter [Greek, Petros—a large piece of rock], and on this rock [Greek, petra—a huge rock like Gibraltar] I will build My church, and the gates*

of Hades (the powers of the infernal region) shall not overpower it [or be strong to its detriment or hold out against it]" (Matthew 16:18).

God expects us to be marching against the forces of evil and overcoming them and He gave us the authority to do it! It is called **dunamis** and it flows to us from the resurrection of Christ. Philippians 3:10 says, *"that I may know Him, and the power of His resurrection ..."* (KJV). Here, the apostle Paul says there is a power that comes from the resurrection. The word translated as "power" here is the Greek word "dunamis".

What is so special about this power that Paul considered it second in importance to knowing Christ Himself? The word "dunamis" means in Greek, "power for performing miracles" and **"excellence of soul."**[4] Wow! No wonder Paul made that bold statement! It is so important, I feel I should repeat it for you. Dunamis is the power that causes miracles in the believer's life and also has the ability to **heal our wounded souls**.

Dunamis is the same power Jesus used to defeat our enemy Satan and every sickness, disease and disorder he uses to attack people. Acts 10:38 says, *"God anointed Jesus of Nazareth with the Holy Ghost and with power* (dunamis): *who went about doing good, and healing all that were oppressed of the devil; for God was with Him"* (KJV). Don't forget what the Bible says, in 3 John 1:2 – that we are prospered and brought in to health *"even as our soul prospers."* When we receive healing in our souls, we get miracles in our finances and in our bodies.

Jesus was anointed with dunamis, which gave Him the power to perform amazing miracles, but because dunamis also means "excellence of soul", it meant that everyone to whom He ministered, was healed of their soul wounds! When He released His anointing of dunamis on them, it caused their souls to become excellent. Then they were prospered and brought into health, even as their souls prospered.

Jesus wasn't the only one to heal people using dunamis. He also gave it to His disciples and it empowered them to do signs, wonders and miracles.

The book of Matthew says,
"And Jesus summoned to Him His twelve disciples and gave them power (dunamis) and authority over unclean spirits, to drive them out, and to cure all kinds of disease and all kinds of weakness and infirmity" (Matthew 10:1).

As soon as Jesus imparted dunamis to the disciples, He immediately commanded them to, *"Cure the sick, raise the dead, cleanse the lepers, drive out demons. Freely (without pay) you have received, freely (without charge) give"* (Matthew 10:8). This is dunamis in action. One reason the disciples could heal the diseased, cleanse lepers and drive out demons was because they had been given the power to make sick people excellent in their souls!

You have dunamis too! It's already living inside of you but you probably didn't know it or know what it could do for you.

Perhaps you've heard about the fellow who took a chain saw back to the hardware store and asked for a refund. "What's wrong with it?" the cashier asked.

"It's terrible," the customer grumbled. "I can't cut a thing with it."

"Well, let me take a look," the cashier said. He pulled the starter cord and the saw roared to life.

The customer jumped back, clapped his hands over his ears in horror and cried, "What's that noise?"

The saw had plenty of power – but it wouldn't help the person who didn't know how to turn it on.

God calls us to live daily within the glory and power of the empty tomb. Without the resurrection, Jesus would still be a man dead in a tomb and the payment He paid for us to be healed of sin and sickness would be dead in the tomb with Him. We need the cross **and** the resurrection.

You already have dunamis power. Now release it! Like the man with the chain saw, you just need to understand how to turn it on and let it work.

Romans 1:16 says,

"For I am not ashamed of the gospel of Christ: for it is the power of God unto salvation to every one that believeth …." (KJV).

Again, the word translated as "power" here is "dunamis".[4] According to this scripture, it was the power that brought about your salvation. This means when you received Jesus as your Lord and Savior, your spirit man was instantly filled with dunamis. So, right now, you have a tank full of soul-healing power already living inside of you! At this very moment you have the power to perform miracles and the ability to be excellent of soul! Now that you understand this, you can release and receive into your soul what you already have. Just as you spend time decreeing the blood over yourself every day, start praying for dunamis to be released into your inner man.

The Apostle Paul wrote:
"May He grant you out of the rich treasury of His glory, to be strengthened and reinforced with mighty power (du-namis) in your inner man by the [Holy] Spirit [Him-self indwelling your innermost being and personality]"
(Ephesians 3:16).

The Strong's concordance says the "inner" man is the "soul"![5] So Paul was praying that your inner man would be filled with dunamis because it would cause you to be strengthened and reinforced in your soul!

Start praying the same way Paul did! Have you been raised to new life with Christ? If so, you have access to His resurrection power.

If you haven't been walking in the dunamis power of the resurrection, you need to start right now:

- Decree that your soul is excellent.
- Pray for God to flood your soul with dunamis.

The more you pray for your soul to be filled with duna-mis, the more you will prosper in every way. In fact you will begin to see your wildest dreams come true!

Ephesians 3:20-21 says,

"Now to Him Who, by (in consequence of) the [action of His] power (dunamis) that is at work within us, is able to [carry out His purpose and] do superabundantly, far

over and above all that we [dare] ask or think [infinitely beyond our highest prayers, desires, thoughts, hopes, or dreams]—To Him be glory in the church and in Christ Jesus throughout all generations forever and ever. Amen (so be it)."

Think about it! According to this verse, God is able to do "superabundantly" more then we could ever ask, imagine or dream according to the dunamis that is at work in our souls. The more we get healed of the wounds inside of us and become excellent of soul, the more we will prosper in our relationships, finances, health and every single area of our lives!

Stop being sick, broke, and having trouble in your marriage. If you're constantly dealing with problems like these, it is most likely because you've only partaken of half of what Jesus did for you. Don't neglect the gift He already gave you!

CHAPTER THREE

THE GLORY AND THE LIGHT

Now when Solomon had made an end of praying, the
fire came down from heaven, and consumed the burnt
offering and the sacrifices; and the glory of the Lord
filled the house. – 2 Chronicles 7:1 KJV

Healing for the wounded soul also comes to us when the glory of the Lord falls on us. I'm talking about the same glory that filled the temple when it was dedicated. Remember, the Bible says that you are the temple of the Holy Spirit (1 Corinthians 6:19). You are a spirit that lives in a body that houses your soul.

Throughout the Bible we read about the glory of the Lord filling the temple. In fact, the scriptures tell us that the glory was so strong on the day that Solomon dedicated the temple that the priests couldn't even enter the temple to perform their duties (2 Chronicles 7:1,2).

TAKING REFUGE UNDER GOD'S WINGS

God's glory **always** fills the temple and it has the power to heal our souls. Let me explain. The prophet Malachi says, *"But unto you who revere and worshipfully fear My name shall the Sun of Righteousness arise with healing in His wings and His beams, and you shall go forth and gambol like calves [released] from the stall and leap for joy"* (Malachi 4:2).

According to this scripture, Jesus, who is the **son of righteousness**, heals us using two powers, "His wings and His beams". The beams represent His light, which we'll talk about in a minute, but what do the wings represent?

The author of Hebrews writes, *"Above [the ark] and overshadowing the mercy seat were the representations of the cherubim [**winged creatures which were the symbols**] of glory"* (Hebrews 9:5, EMPHASIS ADDED) According to this verse, the wings represent God's glory. As I mentioned earlier, the glory of God always fills the temple – and when Jesus arises on us with healing in His wings, His glory has the power to heal our wounded souls. Read through the Psalms and you'll find this theme repeated several times as David talks about our souls taking refuge under God's wings. For example:

> *"Be merciful unto me, O God, be merciful unto me: for my soul trusteth in thee: yea, in the shadow of Thy wings will I make my refuge, until these calamities be overpast"* (Psalm 57:1 KJV).

David said that his soul found refuge under the shadow of God's wings, which is His glory. He had many wounds in his soul from the traumas he experienced while being chased by Saul. He was also wounded by the sin of adultery he committed with Bathsheba and the murder of her husband, Uriah the Hittite. David desperately needed healing in his soul, which is why he sought shelter under the shadow of God's wings. Look at Malachi 4:2 again. This passage says that Jesus *"arises on us with healing in His wings."* The glory is one of the ways God heals our wounded souls.

The Apostle Paul writes, *"And all of us, as with unveiled face, [because we] continued to behold [in the Word of God] as in a mirror the glory of the Lord, are constantly being transfigured into His very own image in ever increasing splendor and from one degree of glory to another ..."* (2 Corinthians 3:18). In this passage, Paul is not speaking about our spirits being progressively healed from glory to glory. Our spirits are transformed and made perfect in an instant. He is referring to our souls being healed step by step through the power of God's glory.

There are three reasons why I know that the glory of God heals.

1. It says so in scripture.
2. I have experienced it myself. It's not a theory to me. It's reality.
3. I have seen thousands of other people being healed in their physical bodies and every area of their lives when their souls were healed in the glory.

BRINGING THE GLORY OF GOD

How do you get the glory to come? The answer is that the glory of God comes from both inside and outside of you. Let me explain.

First, believe it or not, you already possess the glory of God! In John 17:22 Jesus says, "*I have given to them the glory and honor which You have given Me, that they may be one [even] as We are one.*"

This means that Jesus has already given us His glory! Just like dunamis, it lives inside our born-again, perfected spirit man! You already have a tank full of glory. Now you just need to use it. You can command the glory that is in your spirit man to flow into the wounded parts of your soul to cause you to be transformed into His image and His likeness.

God's glory also will come to you externally when you are caught up in worship, and pressing in to get closer to Him. As you praise Him and exalt His name, you will feel His presence increasing. It's during those moments that your soul will find refuge under the shadow of His wings.

It can happen anywhere. It could be that you're praising Him in church on a Sunday morning when the glory falls. Or it could happen while you're listening to praise music and cleaning the house. Or perhaps you're worshiping Him in your car while you're on the way to work and you suddenly realize that He's in the car with you!

There's exhilaration when the glory comes, a divine dizziness that feels very much like the light-headed feeling you get when you fall in love. The glory will also cause your mind to be quiet. Suddenly, all that mind noise and demonic chatter will cease. There is also a weight that accompanies the arrival of the glory. The root of the word "glory" in Hebrew is the word *Kabod*. It actually means "weighty".[6] Sometimes your shoulders might feel a weight on them when the glory comes. Other times, it will be so heavy that you can't get up from the floor. You might even feel an overwhelming urge to go to sleep. Don't worry. It's not the devil. It's the Lord putting you in a place of deep rest so He can heal your soul. In that moment, God is there with healing for your inner man. Don't let the moment pass. Remind yourself, "The glory is here and my soul is getting healed right now. I decree it!"

I talked earlier about the woman with an issue of blood. She was sick in her body and in her soul because she had been suffering for twelve long years and had *spent all of her living on physicians.*" The Bible says she was healed when she touched the *"border of His garment"*– or, to be more specific, the wings of His prayer shawl (Luke 8:43,44). At that moment, Malachi 4:2 came to pass in her life! *"The Sun of righteousness"*, Jesus, arose on her with healing in His wings! She was healed in her body and soul by the glory.

I believe her soul was wounded by the trauma she went through while trying to get healed. Notice that when she touched the hem of Jesus' garment, the Bible says He felt "power" coming out of Him to heal her (v. 46). That word translated as "power" here is "dunamis"![4] Dunamis is made up of the glory of God and they both do the same thing, which is to heal your wounded soul. That day, the woman with the issue of blood was made excellent of soul. Then she was prospered in her health even as her soul was prospered.

You can have the same thing she received. When you're worshiping God and the glory falls on you, say, "I'm touching those wings. I'm grabbing hold of the border of that holy prayer shawl right now." Then expect God to release His glory on you to heal your wounded soul.

Even when you're having one of those days when nothing seems to be going right and you just want to crawl into bed and hide from the world – turn on the praise music, lift up your hands in worship, and let His glory flow into your house. He will come with healing in His wings and lift you out of your funk. You see, when you earnestly seek God, He comes to you, bringing blessings and benefits. It's as if He says, "I've come in response to your worship, because you pressed in and offered up the sacrifice of praise. And when I show up, you get healed."

THE INWARD PERFECTION OF CHRIST

One of the meanings of the word "glory" is "the absolutely perfect inward or personal excellence of Christ."[7] This is significant, because it is in our inner being – our soul – where we most need healing and perfection. When the glory is released, our Lord's inward perfection is imparted to our inner man.

Now, we must be careful that we're not worshiping God because we want something from Him. Our motives must be pure. We worship God because of who He is. But, at the same time, when we earnestly seek Him, He longs to bless us. One of the ways He does this is through the glory and light of His presence.

THE LIGHT OF CHRIST

Malachi 4:2 says that Jesus also arises with "*healing in His beams.*" The word "beams" there refers to beams of light.

What exactly does this light coming from Christ do? The scripture says it arises on us with "healing", which, according to the Hebrew, means "health, healing, and cure."[8] It also means to be of "sound mind."[8] Your mind is part of your soul. Malachi 4 indicates that Jesus comes with light to heal not just your body, but also your mind and every part of your soul man!

Jesus is the light of the world. He emanates brightness! Hebrews 1:3 tells us that Jesus is *the sole expression of the glory of God [the Light-being, the out-raying or radiance of the divine], and He is the perfect imprint and very image of [God's] nature..."*

According to this scripture, Jesus is literally a Light being! It also says He is the perfect imprint of the very nature of God. So when Christ shines His light in you, it burns God's perfect nature into you!

Christ's light heals you and makes you more like Him because it drives out the darkness in your wounded soul. John 8:12 says, "*Once more Jesus addressed the crowd. He said, I am the Light of the world. **He who follows Me will not be walking in the dark, but will have the Light which is Life**"*(EMPHASIS ADDED). Thayers' gives a great description of the root of the word "dark"; "the soul that has lost its perceptive powers."[9] That is what wounds do to you. They cause you to lose the ability to perceive things correctly. Yet here, Jesus says that He is the light, and when you follow Him, His light will bring life to the dark wounded areas in your inner man!

Jesus came with His light so you would not have to continue being controlled by the darkness in your wounded soul. Let me prove it to you. Read this statement from Jesus in John

12:46: *"I have come as a Light into the world, so that whoever believes in Me [whoever cleaves to and trusts in and relies on Me]* ***may not continue to live in darkness"*** (EMPHASIS ADDED).

Wow! Jesus actually came as a light to this world so that we could be healed and no longer controlled by the darkness in our inner man! In Luke 11:34-36, Jesus says, *"Your eye is the lamp of your body; when your eye (your conscience) is sound and fulfilling its office, your whole body is full of light; but when it is not sound and is not fulfilling its office, your body is full of darkness. Be careful, therefore, that the light that is in you is not darkness. If then your entire body is illuminated, having no part dark, it will be wholly bright [with light], as when a lamp with its bright rays gives you light."*

According to this passage, your eye – or your soul – will not be *"sound"* and *"fulfilling its office,"* if *"your body is full of darkness."* In other words, if you are full of wounds that were created by sin, then you are full of darkness and your mind, your will and emotions will not be fulfilling their offices properly.

This same scripture says that when your whole body is filled with the light of Christ then your eye and your soul man will be completely *"sound and fulfilling its office!"* That means your mind will think right thoughts and make balanced God-directed decisions. When your whole body is filled with light, your emotions will be sound and properly fulfilling their office. God created your emotions. They are supposed to be functioning properly. You are to experience joy and not depression. You can have Holy anger in righteousness but not rage. When all is as it should be, you will experience passion but not lust. According to this scripture, when your whole body is filled with light, then every part of your soul will be sound and fulfilling its office. This includes your will, your ability to choose right and wrong. Your ability to make good decisions will dramatically increase, and thus, so will your success and prosperity in every area of your life!

The Light of Christ has the power to heal your soul man and cause your soul man to be completely sound. Remember, Malachi 4 says *"the Sun of righteousness will arise with healing in His wings and His beams..."*!

RELEASING THE LIGHT OF CHRIST

Again, His light comes from inside you and outside you. The Bible says, *"You are the light of the world"* (Matthew 5:14). You see, when Jesus came to live inside of you; immediately your spirit man was filled with His light!

Acts 26:18 says that when Jesus comes to reside in one of His chosen people it will, *"...open their eyes that they may turn from darkness to light and from the power of Satan to God, so that they may thus receive forgiveness and release from their sins and a place and portion among those who are consecrated and purified by faith in Me."*

When a person is born again, the light of Christ fills them, in order to empower them to be healed of the darkness in them that Satan is using to control them. Right now, your spirit man is full of dunamis, glory and light! You have a tank full inside of you that you can release anytime, through prayer and decrees, to get healing for your wounded soul!

As is true with the glory, the light of Christ also comes

upon you externally, through praise and worship. In fact the Bible says the glory cloud is made up of light! When Jesus was on the mount of transfiguration, the scripture says that *"a shining cloud [composed of light] overshadowed them..."* (Matthew 17:5).

When that glory cloud composed of light showed up, it caused Jesus to be completely covered with Heaven's blazing light! Matthew 17:2 says, *"And His appearance underwent a change in their presence; and His face shone clear and bright like the sun, and His clothing became as white as light."*

Mark 9:2-3 says Jesus was, *"...transfigured before them and became resplendent with divine brightness. And His garments became glistening, intensely white, as no fuller (cloth dresser, launderer) on earth could bleach them."*

I have had many encounters that reminded me of the day Jesus was covered with light on the Mount of Transfiguration. There have been dozens of times when, during my praise and worship, I've been covered with so much Christ-Light that my skin actually turned red, like a sun burn!

When you praise God, this is what happens! The word "praise" in the Old Testament means "to shine forth light!"[10]

Begin to release the Light of Christ in you through decrees and around you through praise and worship, and watch your soul get massive healing!

CHAPTER FOUR

GRACE

*For out of His fullness (abundance) we have all received
[all had a share and we were all supplied with] one
grace after another and spiritual blessing upon spiritual
blessing and even favor upon favor and gift [heaped]
upon gift.* – John 1:16

One of the coolest things in the universe is the power of
grace. Lately, I've noticed, within the body of Christ, there
has been a lot of talk concerning this profound subject. Yet I
hear very little about the ability of grace to heal our wounded
souls! According to its meaning, grace was built by God for
just such a purpose.

Look at the word "grace" in the Strong's Concordance:
"The merciful kindness by which God, exerting his holy influence upon souls, turns them to Christ, keeps, strengthens,
increases them in Christian faith, knowledge, affection, and
kindles them to the exercise of the Christian virtues."[11]

Did you catch all of that? Grace is a soul-healing power! It
is a "holy influence" that "keeps" the soul, "strengthens" and
"increases" it. Grace also "kindles" the soul to the exercise of

Christian virtues, meaning grace gives you the power to act right because it heals the wounds in your soul that are the cause of your attitude problems. Grace is much more than a doctrine. It is a literal power that can heal all the wounded areas inside of you that are sabotaging every part of your existence.

There are things in your inner man that are driving you to sin against yourself, others and God. You may realize these behaviors and addictions need to be eradicated, yet some are so strong they seem impossible to shake. That's what soul wounds do. They control you and cause you to sin. Romans 5:20 says, "...*where sin increased and abounded, grace, (God's unmerited favor) has surpassed it and increased the more and even superabounded...*" When the sin in your soul increases, God's grace, His unmerited favor, surpasses the sin, increasing even more and even super-abounding over it!

I think the church, as a whole, is under the wrong impression about grace. I have heard a lot of people say, when we sin, grace covers it. I understand what they mean, however, what people really need to realize is that grace *keeps the soul, strengthens and increases* it*, and kindles the soul to the exercise of Christian virtues.* Grace doesn't just *cover* over your sin, **it heals your soul, so that you won't want to sin anymore**!

What I love most about grace is that it is free! You received an unending supply once you were born again in Christ. Ephesians 2:5 says, *"Even when we were dead (slain) by [our own] shortcomings and trespasses, He made us alive together in fellowship and in union with Christ; [He gave us the very life of Christ Himself, the same new life with which He quickened Him, for]* **it is by grace (His favor and mercy which you did not deserve) that you are saved (delivered from judgment and made partakers of Christ's salvation)"** (EMPHASIS ADDED).

Grace is undeserved (couldn't earn it, couldn't buy it) it's totally free favor and mercy from God. God's grace is so awesome that He poured it out on you even when you were dead in your sins and a hater of God! The reason you are now saved and given a whole new life in Christ is because of God's free grace.

And that is only the beginning. Once you belong to Jesus, His grace keeps flowing unendingly into your life, filling your soul to heal you, deliver you and change you into His likeness.

The Bible says that we will prosper and be in health even as our soul prospers (see 3 John 1:2). As your soul is healed, you prosper in every other area, including your finances and your health. Prosperity of soul causes God's promises to come to pass in your life! The exciting news is that God's free grace makes this happen because it heals your soul! The more you understand grace and appropriate what you already have, the more healing you will receive in your inner man and that is when you will prosper and be in health in every area.

Look at this amazing verse in Romans 4, *"Therefore, [inheriting] the promise is the outcome of faith and depends [entirely] on faith in order that it may be given as an act of grace..."* (verse 16).

According to the Bible, the way you inherited all of God's promises is by grace, through your faith! I have heard people teach this verse from many different perspectives. However, they did not connect all the dots; grace heals your soul, **which then causes you to prosper!**

Trust and believe, as grace fills your soul, you will see an explosion of God's promises in your life!

Now, notice the verse in Romans 4 says that it is grace through your faith that you inherit the promises. I think a lot of people have been trying to do too much in their own strength to make their promises happen instead of believing in God's grace. I love grace because it brings balance and rest to the exhausted body of Christ. I believe many of us are stuck in a rut, thinking we need to earn our breakthroughs. When stuff doesn't happen, how and when we expect, we wrongly assume we did something wrong or that we didn't do enough. Yet, Romans 4 tells us that we will inherit all the promises, not through our own works or efforts, but rather from grace through our faith.

Don't get me wrong. There are things we should do to partner with God to cause the full manifestation of His word. Jesus spoke of this, using phrases such as, *"When you fast..."* and *"this kind comes out through prayer and fasting"* (see Matthew 6:16 and Mark 9:29) He even said, *"Repent for the kingdom of heaven is at hand"* meaning when we repent, fast and pray it causes the kingdom to manifest in our lives (see Matthew 3:2). So, Jesus Himself said that we need to do these things. Yet even when we are instructed by Holy Spirit to take certain steps of obedience, it is still only by His grace that they work.

So what should you do? Just let grace alone accomplish everything for you or combine your acts of obedience with grace? The key to attaining balance between these two seemingly opposing positions is to be led by the spirit of the Lord.

Do only what He leads you to do. Jesus said He only did what He saw the Father doing and He was successful in everything (see John 5:19)! He was always led by the Father, so He never did any dead works, but He also didn't just stand around and let the power of grace do it all. The Bible says He was full of *both* grace and truth. Jesus said He was always busy *doing* the Father's *works*! He worked and partnered with God in all things and the grace of the Lord was with totally Him.

There was a time when I was tired and burned out from trying to make things happen in my life. That is when God first started teaching me about grace. I was trying so hard to get my soul healed, so my promises would manifest. In that process, I stepped out of grace. I crossed the line from being led by the Holy Spirit to relying on my own strength to make stuff happen. Unfortunately, the more works I did, the worse my situation became. I was acting up more, getting sicker and basically losing it. That's when God showed me a scripture that explained why that was happening. Galatians 3:10 says *"And for all who depend on the law, [who are seeking to be justified by obedience to the law of rituals] are under a curse and doomed to disappointment..."* I had fallen into a bad habit of keeping fleshly rituals in an effort to see my breakthrough. I fasted excessively even though the Holy Spirit hadn't led me to do so and I repented endlessly for every little mistake. Jesus told us to fast and repent but I had let those graces turn into legalistic rituals that I was using to become "holy". But only Jesus makes us holy, by grace through our faith, not our works. When we cross over from doing good acts of obedience into keeping excessive legalistic rituals, we will literally be cursed! No wonder things were getting so bad for me.

The Bible says that we are made the righteousness of God through Christ if we will just believe. Grace is a power that makes you righteous! It keeps your soul and strengthens your soul and it's free. Then you will inherit your promises!

How do you do that? Ephesians 2:8 says that it is by grace through faith that you are saved. Your faith releases grace. The more faith you have, the more grace will be active in your life. So how do you get more faith? You grow it!

The Bible says, *"faith comes by hearing and hearing by the word of God"* (Romans 10:17). When you study, meditate on and decree the word of God, it increases and grows your faith. One of the reasons why this little book is so powerful is because it's full of the Word of God! Every time you read one of the decrees contained here, it will cause your faith to rise for healing and deliverance. When your faith rises, then grace is automatically released! When that happens, grace also flows into your soul to bring you even more healing!

The more teaching and Word you hear about grace, the more it will pour into your life until you become what the Bible calls *"full of grace"*! John 1:14 says this about Jesus, "*[The Word Becomes Flesh] And the Word became flesh and dwelt among us, and we beheld His glory, the glory as of the only begotten of the Father, **full of grace** and truth"* (EMPHASIS ADDED). Jesus is full of grace! Do you know why? Look at the above verse again. **It's because He is the Word!!**

Grace is released through your faith and faith comes by hearing and hearing by the Word! Study grace scriptures, meditate on them and decree them. Then the Word will cause you to be like Jesus, *full of grace!*

Miracles happen when you are *full of grace!* In Acts 6:8 it says, *"Now Stephen, **full of grace** (divine blessing and favor) and power (strength and ability) **worked great wonders and signs (miracles) among the people"** (EMPHASIS ADDED).

Wow! Because Stephen was *full of grace* and power, he could work great wonders, signs and miracles among the people. What does it mean to be *full of grace?* When I looked up the word "full" in the Strong's, I almost jumped out of my skin! It means, to be "thoroughly permeated in the soul." [12] Stephen understood grace so much that he was *full* of grace. Literally, his soul was saturated with grace and it was doing what grace does; keeping his soul, strengthening his soul, increasing his soul, causing his soul to be controlled by Christian virtues. No wonder he could do so many miracles! He was thoroughly permeated in his soul with the power of grace!

As you saturate yourself with the word of grace, you'll become like Stephen, full of grace. As your soul gets permeated with grace, you'll start to see physical miracles happening, just like he did!

Listen to the grace word preached, meditate on it and decree it. Your faith will grow to receive even more grace. As that faith rises up in you, then grace will be released even more into your soul and every area of your life!

Now make these decrees to appropriate your healing and miracles in your life through the power of grace!

I decree that I am saved and born again because of grace by faith. (Ephesians 2:8-9)

I decree sin shall not have dominion over me, for I am not under the law, but under grace. Grace is healing every area in my soul that has been controlling me. Grace is a *holy influence* that *keeps my soul, strengthens my soul and increases my soul.* Grace is *kindling my soul to be controlled by Christian virtues.* Grace is healing my soul, so that I will not sin. Sin will not have dominion over me because I will not desire to sin anymore. (Romans 6:14)

I decree healing to the areas in my soul that are driving me to have addictions, attitude problems or are causing me to partake of things that I should not. I know that where sin increases and abounds, grace, God's unmerited favor has surpassed it and increased the more and even **superabounded**. Grace is healing my soul and delivering me of all attitudes and addictions in Jesus name! (Romans 5:20)

I decree Holy Spirit will give me discernment to show me when I have gone from Holy Spirit inspired acts of obedience to works that are dead, have no oil on them, and are not full of grace. I break off every curse now that came upon me through the keeping of the law of rituals. I decree I am free of those curses because I am under grace. (Romans 4:16, Galatians 3:10)

I decree that I am growing my faith by hearing the word of God. As I read, listen, and speak the words of Christ, my faith will grow and that will cause grace to be released into my soul. I decree I am becoming like Stephen, full of grace! I am thoroughly permeated in my soul with the power of grace! I am full of grace so I will see and perform great wonders, signs and miracles among the people, just as Stephen did! (Romans 10:17, Acts 6:8)

Now declare these powerful grace scriptures:

John 1:16 - *"For out of His fullness (abundance) we have all received [all had a share and we were all supplied with] one grace after another and spiritual blessing upon spiritual blessing and even favor upon favor and gift [heaped] upon gift."*

Romans 4:16 - *"Therefore [inheriting] the promise is the outcome of faith and depends [entirely] on faith in order that the promise may be given as an act of grace (unmerited favor)..."*

Romans 5:2 - *"Through Him also we have [our] access (entrance, introduction) by faith into this grace (state of God's favor) in which we [firmly and safely] stand. And let us rejoice and exult in our hope of experiencing and enjoying the glory of God."*

Romans 16:20 - *"And the God of peace will soon crush Satan under your feet. The grace of our Lord Jesus Christ (the Messiah) be with you."*

2 Corinthians 8:9 - *"For you are becoming progressively acquainted with and recognizing more strongly and clearly the grace of our Lord Jesus Christ (His kindness, His gracious generosity, His undeserved favor and spiritual blessing), [in] that though He was [so very] rich, yet for your sakes He became [so very] poor, in order that by His poverty you might become enriched (abundantly supplied)."*

2 Corinthians 9:8 - *"And God is able to make all grace (every favor and earthly blessing) come to you in abundance, so that you may always and under all circumstances and whatever the need be self-sufficient [possessing enough to require no aid or support and furnished in abundance for every good work and charitable donation]."*

Galatians 2:21 - *"[Therefore, I do not treat God's gracious gift as something of minor importance and defeat its very purpose]; I do not set aside and invalidate and frustrate and nullify the grace (unmerited favor) of God. For if justification (righteous- ness, acquittal from guilt) comes through [observing the ritual of] the Law, then Christ (the Messiah) died groundlessly and to no purpose and in vain. [His death was then wholly superfluous.]"*

Titus 2:11-12 - *"For the grace of God (His unmerited favor and blessing) has come forward (appeared) for the deliverance from sin and the eternal salvation for all mankind. It has trained us to reject and renounce all ungodliness (irreligion) and worldly (passionate) desires, to live discreet (temperate, self-controlled), upright, devout (spiritually whole) lives in this present world."*

1 Peter 1:2 - *"Who were chosen and foreknown by God the Father and consecrated (sanctified, made holy) by the Spirit to be obedi- ent to Jesus Christ (the Messiah) and to be sprinkled with [His] blood: May grace (spiritual blessing) and peace be given you in increasing abundance [that spiritual peace to be realized in and through Christ, freedom from fears, agitating passions, and moral conflicts]."*

1 Peter 5:10 - *"And after you have suffered a little while, the God of all grace [Who imparts all blessing and favor], Who has called you to His [own] eternal glory in Christ Jesus, will Himself complete and make you what you ought to be, establish and ground you securely, and strengthen, and settle you."*

CHAPTER FIVE

DECREES TO HEAL THE WOUNDED SOUL

Over the next several chapters, I am going to take you through a number of decrees that will bring you supernatural strength, heal your wounded soul, and enable you to live in the dunamis power of Christ's resurrection. Healing and might will flow into you as you read, pray and speak these words.

In this chapter, you will speak decrees related to the blood of Jesus to wash away every sin that has wounded your soul. In the pages ahead, we'll deal with specific areas of need, including decrees to:

- Release dunamis into your soul and body.
- Establish the healing power of God's glory and His light.
- Overcome offenses.
- Overcome the traumas that are holding you back from living life to the fullest.
- Defeat the kingdom of darkness.

Think of these decrees as being like antibiotics for your soul. Have you ever had an illness that came back because you didn't take all the medicine your doctor prescribed? You were supposed to take one pill a day for ten days, but quit after five because you were feeling so much better. Then the illness came back, perhaps even worse than before. Don't make that mistake here. Meditate on these words. Focus on them. Read them over and over until they become an absolute reality to you. As you speak these decrees to heal the wounded soul, keep these three important Scriptures in mind:

> *"Receive and welcome the Word which implanted and rooted [in your hearts] contains the power to save your souls"* (James 1:21).

> *"Thou shalt also decree a thing, and it shall be established unto thee: and the light shall shine upon thy ways"* (Job 22:28, KJV).

> *As the rain and the snow come down from heaven, and do not return to it without watering the earth and making it bud and flourish, so that it yields seed for the sower and bread for the eater,so is my word that goes out from my mouth: It will not return to me empty, but will accomplish what I desire and achieve the purpose for which I sent it"* (Isaiah 55:10-11, NIV).

These words are full of power, they work and they will change your life!

There is only one place to start, with the precious blood of Jesus. His blood is the entryway into all the blessings God has in store for us.

CLEANSING THE ANCIENT GATES

In Psalm 24, verses 7 through 10, David writes:

> *"Lift up your heads, you gates;*
> *be lifted up, you ancient doors,*
> *that the King of glory may come in.*
> *Who is this King of glory?*
> *The Lord strong and mighty,*
> *he Lord mighty in battle.*
> *Lift up your heads, you gates;*
> *lift them up you, you ancient doors,*
> *that the King of glory may come in.*
> *Who is He, this King of glory?*
> *The Lord Almighty –*
> *He is the King of glory"*(NIV).

When David wrote about the gates and ancient doors, he was talking about the entrances to the temple in Jerusalem. Today, God's temple is within the hearts and souls of His people. In other words, we are His temple, but there are ancient gates in our souls that have been slammed shut because our ancestors sinned. When we apply the blood of Jesus to those gates and then command them to be lifted up, they open so that dunamis, glory and light can flow into our souls. You can use the following decrees to ensure that you have covered every gate with the blood of Jesus.

I release the blood of Jesus onto the gates of my mind, my conscious and sub-conscious, my thoughts, reasoning, intellect, imagination and understanding. I repent of any sinful thoughts I have allowed myself to meditate on or any indecent, evil image I have created in my imagination. I believe I am being washed clean and forgiven of every sin connected to every part of my mind. I decree that all the ancient gates inside my mind are being opened right now by the blood of Jesus! (2 Corinthians10:5, Psalm 51:1-2)

I command the ancient gates in my soul that are connected to my will to be covered with the blood of Jesus. I repent of any time I used my will to make wrong, destructive, hurtful choices. I believe every sin I ever committed with my will is being healed right now! Because of Jesus' all-powerful sacrifice, the gates and doors to my will are being opened now. My will is being healed and I decree, from now on, I will make right, healthy decisions. (1 John 1:7-9)

I decree that Jesus Christ is my Lord and Savior and that every ancient gate connected to my emotions is being opened now. I send the blood to the gates of my passions, desires, appetites, and emotions. I command those gates to be lifted up right now by the power of His blood. I repent of any time I sinned with my emotions by allowing myself to get angry, feel depressed or anxious and fearful. I ask for forgiveness for every negative emotion I allowed myself to feel. I repent of acting on any unholy, unrighteous passions and I decree that my passions are being washed and purified in the blood of Jesus. I also repent of any time I allowed myself to be controlled by any unholy appetites. I apply the blood of Jesus to any appetites that were of the world and not of the kingdom of God. (1 Corinthians 6:11, James 1:19-21)

I decree that the gates to my emotions, passions and appetites are being opened by the blood of Jesus and I am being healed in every area of this part of my soul. I decree I only feel good, God-given emotions. My passions will be directed toward the Lord. My desires will be for the things of Him. My appetites will not be for the things of the world but for things that are healthy, wholesome and holy. (Galatians 5:24, Titus 2:12)

I command every ancient gate inside my body to be covered by the blood of Jesus and to be open in His holy name. I apply the blood of Jesus to my eye gate, my ear gate, my mouth gate, my nose gate and my touch gate. I repent for any evil thing I allowed my eye to look upon, including all violence, coveting and unclean television and movie viewing. I put the blood of Jesus on my ear gate and I repent of any lie, gossip, or wicked thing that I allowed myself to listen to. I repent for any evil, slanderous, bitter, negative, grumbling, cursing word that I allowed to come out of my mouth gate. I apply the blood of Jesus to my nose gate to wash it clean of any sin – including every kind of drug abuse, criticizing any unpleasant smells coming from another person or environment, thus hurting and wounding people, and allowing smells that came through my nose gate to entice me into sexual sin or even drive me to eat more than I should. I also repent of any sins I committed with my touch gate, including all fornication, lust and perversion. I also forgive anyone who sinned against my touch gate by touching me in an unsanctified sexual manner, including molestation, rape and abuse of any kind. I decree the blood of Jesus is covering every one of my body gates and they are all being opened so that dunamis power and the glory and light of

Christ can flow into my physical body and heal me. I believe, as these gates are opened and healed, I will have physical miracles as well as be able to see in the spirit better, hear God's voice clearer, speak His Word with accuracy and power, smell the fragrance of His presence and sense His touch in a new level. (Ephesians 4:25-32, Ecclesiastes 5:1-3, Psalm 119:37, James 1:19)

I decree the truth of Leviticus 17 that the Blood atones for my soul. I release the blood of Jesus to atone, cover and completely remove every sin that ever wounded my soul. (Leviticus 17:11)

I decree that Jesus Christ is my Lord and Savior and that every stain on my soul, from sins I've committed, has been washed away by His blood. I have redemption through His blood, the forgiveness of sins, in accordance with the riches of God's grace that He lavished on me. Although, I was once far away from God, I have been brought near to Him through the blood of Christ. (Ephesians 1:7, 2:13)

Through the blood Jesus shed on Calvary, I have been set free from the law of sin and death. Because I am covered with the blood of Jesus, when God looks at my soul, He sees only the righteousness of His only Son. (Romans 8:2, 2 Corinthians 5:21)

Jesus shed His blood for me and I am a new creation in Him. I am no longer tainted by my own sins, whether they were committed willfully or in ignorance. Because of the blood of Jesus, I do not have to receive or believe any condemnation or accusations from the enemy. Jesus made a public spectacle of the enemy at the cross. At the cross, Jesus became a curse for me, thus breaking the power of every curse that would try to beset my body and my soul. His blood demolished the law of sin and death over me and now I have life abundant here and now. (2 Corinthians 5:17, Galatians 3:3, Romans 8:1-4)

Through the blood and grace of Jesus, I have been set free from the guilt and shame of sins in my soul that have been passed down through the generations from my earthly family. I repent for every generational iniquity done by my ancestors and myself. I utterly repent of, and turn away from and renounce, all ungodly practices, sins and iniquities in my family bloodline. I confess and renounce all idolatry, demon worship, Satanism, witchcraft, and occultism. In the name of Jesus Christ, I cover the sins in my soul that were passed down through my family line with the blood of Jesus. I break and renounce all blood sacrifices, blood oaths, blood covenants, blood dedications, blood ties and all blood bondages to Satan and any other false gods by my family and myself. (Romans 6:18, 1 John 1:9, Deuteronomy 18:10-13, Galatians 5:19-24)

I decree that the blood of Jesus is saturating my soul and breaking me free of any ungodly documents, agreements and assignments against me and my family, past, present and future. I apply the blood of Jesus Christ to cancel and divorce them from my body and soul. I declare their penalty has been paid in full by Jesus at Calvary. (Colossians 2:13-14, Romans 4:25 and 3:24)

I confess and repent of all ungodly character bents, behaviors and mental strongholds in my soul that were passed down to me through my family line all the way back to Adam. (1 Corinthians 15:21-22, Romans 5:19)

I repent of all word curses spoken by me or anyone in my bloodline and I put the blood of Jesus on any curses spoken against anyone in any generation. The Bible says the cause-less curse cannot alight. I decree my soul is being washed and healed of every single generational curse and I command every curse on my body and soul to be broken. (Proverbs 26:2, Psalm 103:3, Galatians 3:13)

I confess any addictions in my family bloodlines and I decree that the blood of Jesus is washing away any sins of addiction in my soul that are controlling me now. (1 Corinthians 6:9-11, Hebrews 10:22)

I confess and renounce all wrong doctrinal thinking that may be coming from my soul. My spirit man is filled with Christ, so in my spirit I have perfect doctrine. I command my soul to line up with my spirit in the name of Jesus. (Titus 2:1, 1 Thessalonians 5:23, Ephesians 5:18)

I renounce any hereditary illness, whether physical, emotional or mental and any other weakness in my family bloodlines. I decree the blood of Jesus is washing me clean of any sin in my soul that was passed down through my bloodline and would allow generational sickness to come upon me. I decree that I am being brought into health even as my soul is prospered. (1 John 1:7-9, 3 John 1:2, Revelation 1:5)

I confess and ask forgiveness on my part or on the part of my ancestors for stealing from God by not bringing Him the whole tithe. I decree the blood of Jesus is washing my soul clean of those sins and I am being prospered even as my soul prospers. (Malachi 3:10, Colossians 1:14, 3 John 1:2)

I repent of any ungodly soul ties with a person or a thing. In the name of Jesus Christ I put the blood on every sin in my soul that allowed an unholy soul tie to form in me. I decree that these soul ties are broken in the name of Jesus. (1 Corinthians 6:16-20, 2 Corinthians 6:14-18)

I decree that I will walk daily in the protection and blessing provided through Christ's blood. His blood will cover my hands so they may be useful to Him, and my feet so that I may walk in His footsteps. I decree that His blood will cover my inner man so my thoughts, choices and emotions will be pleasing to Him. (1 Peter 2:21, Hebrews 9:14, Psalm 19:14)

CHAPTER SIX

DECREES TO LOOSE DUNAMIS POWER

Did you know that you received a full supply of dunamis power when you were born again? You already have a tank full of it. Now you just need to believe it and release it!

The Apostle Paul writes, *"And God hath both raised up the Lord, and will also raise up us by his own power"* (1 Corinthians 6:14, KJV). The word "power" here, again, is the word "duna-mis".[4] So according to this verse, God is using the same power He used to raise Christ from the dead to raise us up out of our dead and wounded state!

Let's make some decrees that will release the power you already have in your spirit into your wounded soul.

I release dunamis power into my soul right now. I command the power from the resurrection that fills my spirit man to flow through the ripped veil into every ancient gate in my soul and my body. (Romans 8:11)

I decree that my soul is being filled with dunamis power, the same mighty strength God exerted when He raised Christ from the dead. Through this power I am being conformed into His likeness, according to Romans 8:29. I am being made excellent of soul, and will live daily in the glorious presence of His love and blessing.

Every wound in my soul is being healed right now through the dunamis power of God, which He gives freely to me as His child. In the name of Jesus and through the power of the Holy Spirit, I decree that every weak place in my inner man is being made strong. Every open wound is healing. Every scar is disappearing forever. (Matthew 10:1)

The Lord is refreshing my soul and guiding me in everything I do as I walk in the daily reality of the 23rd Psalm. Blessings and miracles will be my portion. He will restore my soul, then surely goodness and love will follow me all the days of my life, and I will dwell in the house of the Lord forever.

My soul rejoices in my God. "*For he has clothed me with garments of salvation and arrayed me in a robe of his righteousness, as a bridegroom adorns his head like a priest, and as a bride adorns herself with her jewels*" (Isaiah 61:10 NIV).

My body is the temple of God and it houses my spirit, which is filled with dunamis power. I am a vessel of His righteousness. I release that power into the rest of my temple and decree that I have nothing in common with wickedness or fellowship with darkness. Through the power of God, I am able to resist the devil and he must flee from me. (2 Corinthians 6:15 and James 4:7)

I decree that my soul is being filled with the fullness of God, who is able to do immeasurably more than all I ask or imagine according to His power (dunamis) that is at work within me. (Ephesians 3:19-20)

I decree that I am God's workmanship and the temple of His Holy Spirit. When God looks at my soul, He sees the righteousness of His Son, Jesus Christ. I do not have to be held captive by the wounds of the past, for *"there is now no condemnation for those who are in Christ Jesus, because through Christ Jesus the law of the Spirit who gives life has set you free from the law of sin and death"* (Romans 8:1-2 NIV; Ephesians 2:10, 1 Corinthians 3:16)

I decree that my soul is continually filled with joy and the Holy Spirit. Let the peace, soul harmony which comes from Christ rule in my heart, deciding and settling with finality all questions that arise in my mind, keeping me in that peaceful state to which Christ calls me to live. (Colossians 3:15, Acts 13:52)

I pray what Paul prayed in Ephesians 3:16, God grant me out of the rich treasury of Your glory to be strengthened and reinforced with mighty power (dunamis) in my inner man by the Holy Spirit, Himself indwelling my innermost being and personality. I decree that I am being strengthened and reinforced with dunamis in my soul right now. In Jesus' name.

I decree that because I have the same dunamis power the disciples had, I have authority over unclean spirits, to drive them out and to cure all kinds of weakness and infirmity. I will walk in signs and wonders and fulfill Jesus' commandment to, *"Cure the sick, raise the dead, cleanse the lepers, drive out demons!"* Freely, without pay, I have received, freely, without charge, I will give. (Matthew 10:8, Luke 9:1)

CHAPTER SEVEN

DECREES THAT LOOSE LIGHT AND GLORY

Has it been some time since you've experienced God's glory in a powerful way? If so, you need to spend more time in His presence. Put on some praise and worship music and lift your hands and your heart to the Lord. Thank Him for all the wonderful blessings He gives you every day. Praise Him for giving His Son for you so that you can have eternal life in heaven and be totally healed while on earth. The Bible says His presence inhabits our praise (see Psalm 22:3). As you lift your heart to Him in worship, His presence, which is His glory, will come – and so will power to heal your soul!

As you lift your voice in praise, His light will begin to increase and shine into your heart. The word "praise" means to "shine forth light!"[10] So the more you thank Him and praise Him, the more healing you will receive!

Make these decrees while you are in His presence:

Jesus said, *"I have given to them the same glory and honor which You have given Me…"* I decree that I already have the glory Jesus gave to me and now I release it into every soul wound in my inner man. I believe my inner man is being healed right now in Jesus name, according to John 17:22.

I decree that I have lifted up the ancient doors and gates in my soul and body so that the King of Glory may come in and heal me. I am in the presence of the Lord strong and mighty, the Lord mighty in battle. The God of Abraham, Isaac and Jacob is here with me now. The One who parted the Red Sea for the children of Israel, protected Daniel in the lion's den and raised His Son, Jesus Christ, from the dead is here with me right now. He is more than able to heal every wound in my soul by the power of His glory! (Psalm 24:7-10)

I decree that the Sun of righteousness is rising on me right now with healing in His wings. His glory is healing me in my mind, will, emotions and my physical body. I am touching the wings of His prayer shawl like the woman with the issue of blood, so I am being totally healed of every affliction in both soul and body! (Malachi 4:2, Mark 5:25-34)

I decree that You, O Lord, are keeping my soul as the apple of your eye. I believe you are healing my soul under the shadow of your wings. Your glory is keeping me *"from the wicked that oppress me, from my deadly enemies, who compass me about"* (Psalm 17:7-13, KJV).

I decree Psalm 36 over myself. *"How precious is Your steadfast love, O God!"* I *"take refuge and put my trust under the shadow of Your wings."* I *"relish and feast on the abundance of Your house; and You cause them* (me) *to drink of the stream of Your pleasures"* (Psalm 36:7-8).

I speak Psalm 57:1 over my life. *"Be merciful and gracious to me, O God, be merciful and gracious to me, for my soul takes refuge and finds shelter and confidence in You; yes, in the shadow of Your wings will I take refuge and be confident until calamities and destructive storms are passed."*

I believe and decree Psalm 91 that you are my help in times of trouble and I will rest and rejoice in my healing as my soul resides under the shadow of your wings.

I decree that the same glory that fell on the Mount of Transfiguration is falling on me. It is causing me to be transformed into Christ's image from glory to glory. Every part of my mind, will and emotions is being changed into His image and His likeness, in Jesus' name! Praise the Lord! (Matthew 17:1-2, 2 Corinthians 3:18)

I decree that Jesus is my glory and the lifter of my head. His light and glory are here, and He has empowered me and made me ready for anything and equal to anything; I am self-sufficient in Christ's sufficiency. Because Christ favors me with the glory of His presence, rivers of living water shall flow continuously from my innermost being. (Psalm 3:3, Colossians 1:11, John 7:38)

Oh, Lord, thank you for coming near and quenching my soul, which thirsts for you. I behold your power and your glory, and I will praise you as long as I live. In your name I will lift up my hands. My soul will be satisfied as with the richest of foods; and my lips will sing songs of praise to you. (Psalm 63:1-5)

I decree that the Sun of righteousness, Jesus Christ is rising on me with healing in His beams of Light. I receive the Light of Christ into every part of my soul man and I believe I am being healed by it in my mind, will and emotions. I am being released like a calf from the stall to leap with joy. (Malachi 4:2)

Jesus says He is the light of the world and whoever follows Him will not walk in the dark but will have the light which is life. I decree I am not filled with darkness anymore. I am filled with the light of Christ, so I have life. The word "darkness" is described as "the soul that has lost its perceptive powers."[9] I command the light of Jesus to flow into every area of my soul that has lost its ability to perceive correctly. I am being healed now in my thinking, my will and my emotions by His beams of light. (John 8:12)

I decree that God has called me out of darkness and into His marvelous light. I am part of a chosen race, a royal priesthood, a dedicated nation, God's own purchased, special people, that I may set forth His wonderful deeds and display His virtues and perfections. (1 Peter 2:9)

God has rescued me from darkness and brought me into the kingdom of His Son. I was once darkness, but now I am light in the Lord, and I live as a child of the light. My soul is filled with the light of Christ so I have nothing to do with the fruitless deeds of darkness, but rather they have been exposed and healed in me. (Colossians 1:13, Ephesians 5:8-11)

I decree that according to 2 Corinthians 4:6 God is beaming light into my heart so I don't have to live in darkness anymore. *"For God Who said, Let light shine out of darkness, has shone in our hearts so as [to beam forth] the Light for the illumination of the knowledge of the majesty* and *glory of God [as it is manifest in the Person and is revealed] in the face of* Jesus *Christ (the Messiah)."*

CHAPTER EIGHT

DECREES TO OVERCOME OFFENSES

Most of us are easily offended.

And I suspect that some people are offended just because I said so.

We get offended when someone cuts us off in traffic, or when the line is long and the cashier is taking too much time, or because the telemarketer calls during dinnertime.

I admit, all of these things can be annoying, and I could go on to give hundreds of other examples. But God expects us to be compassionate, kind, caring people, and He gives us the power to be what He expects. Furthermore, when we are easily offended, our souls get wounded, then sickness, failure and poverty may be the result.

Recently, I received word from a man who was healed of bone cancer after he heard me speak on this topic. He realized he was carrying around a number of offenses, including many towards his ex-wife. When he applied the blood through repentance and forgiveness, then released dunamis into his soul, his body was healed of that cancer. This is just one example of how important it is to stop being offended.

One of the first things we do when we get offended is speak slanderous, judgmental, angry words about people and circumstances. Little do we realize that these words can literally wound our souls and make us sick.

Proverbs 26:22 says,

"The words of a whisperer or slanderer are like dainty morsels or words of sport [to some, but to others are like deadly wounds]; and they go down into the innermost parts of the body [or of the victim's nature]."

Your words can wound the soul of the person you are talking about, and they can wound yours too, and then make you sick! Use these decrees to overcome offenses:

I repent of speaking evil, slanderous, judgmental and critical words about anyone or anything. I realize my words can cause deadly wounds inside my soul. I believe Jesus is washing me of those sins right now with His blood. I receive the power of the cross to forgive my offenses and I release the dunamis power that is in my spirit to every deadly wound in my soul that came from my words. I decree I am being healed right now, in Jesus' name. (Proverbs 12:18, Psalm 147:3, Revelation 1:5)

I repent for every offended thought I have allowed myself to meditate on. I wash those thoughts out of my mind with the blood of Jesus and I send dunamis power to every wound in my mind that came from thinking offended thoughts. The weapons of my warfare are the blood and the dunamis power and they are mighty for the throwing down of the strongholds of offense in my mind. I will not allow myself to continually think bad or evil about anyone or anything. I take my mind captive to Christ. (1 John 1:7, 2 Corinthians 10:3-5)

I decree through the power of God in my life, my soul is clothed with compassion, kindness, humility, gentleness and patience. In the name of Jesus, I hereby release every grudge and grievance I have been holding. I will forgive as the Lord forgave me, and the peace of Christ will rule in my heart and soul. (Colossians 3:12-15, Ephesians 4:32)

I decree that I refrain from judging others so that I am not judged. According to the dunamis power God has poured into my soul, I do not condemn others or pronounce others guilty, but rather acquit, forgive and release them. In this way, I am acquitted, forgiven and released. (Luke 6:36-38)

My soul is joyful when trials come my way, understanding that God is developing patience and perseverance in me. I decree, I am not easily offended nor do I offend. Day by day, I am growing and maturing in Christ so that I may be complete in Him, not lacking anything. (James 1:2-4, Psalm 119:165)

I decree God's love rules in my heart and soul. I am patient and kind. I do not envy, or boast and I am not proud or self-righteous. I am not rude, self-seeking or easily angered. I do not keep a record of the wrongs done against me. I do not delight in evil but rejoice with the truth. By the grace and power of God, I trust, hope and persevere. (1 Corinthians 13:4-7)

I decree, I will live daily in the reality of the mercy God has shown me by giving His Son to save my soul on the cross of Calvary. Because I am merciful, I obtain mercy. Through the dunamis power within me, I am healed and able to love those who have offended me. I pray for and seek God's blessing for them so I am blessed as I bless others. (Matthew 5:7, 43-44 and 7:1-5)

I decree dunamis power has so healed my soul that I can now manifest the fruit of God's Spirit that lives within me. I am loving, joyful, patient, kind, good, faithful, gentle and I exercise self-control. My sinful nature with its passions and desires has been crucified with Christ. (Romans 6:6, Galatians 2:20 and 5:22-24)

I am the light of the world, and I let my light shine before men, that they may see my good deeds and praise my Father in heaven. My soul is filled with the Light of Christ and it is constantly healing me of all offense. I am the salt of the earth, living at peace with others. My conversation is always full of grace, seasoned with salt, so that others might be drawn to Christ. (Matthew 5:13-16, Mark 9:50, Colossians 4:6)

CHAPTER NINE

DECREES TO OVERCOME TRAUMA

The fifth chapter of Mark tells of Jesus' encounter with a demon-possessed man who lived among tombs. The man, who was possessed by many demons, was so wild that "*no one could bind him anymore, not even with a chain*" (Mark 5:3, NIV).

Of course, the demons were no match for Jesus. He cast them out and they entered into a herd of pigs, which ran into the Sea of Galilee and drowned. I'm sure you're familiar with the story. But what you may not realize is that this man was living the same kind of life that far too many believers experience. They, too, are living among the tombs.

You see, I believe the tombstones in that ancient burial ground were symbolic of the tombs or markers we erect in our own lives because of traumas we've suffered. For example:

"That person betrayed me after I trusted her, so I'm going to erect a tombstone. This other person insulted me, so here is another tombstone. My mother always favored my sister over me, so let me put a tombstone there as well. I was in a severe car accident and I will never get over the trauma I went through."

If we keep focusing and replaying painful events in our lives, pretty soon, we're trapped among those tombs, totally unable to live the powerful, dynamic sort of life God wants for us.

What do we do? First, we've got to tear down the tombstones. They don't serve any purpose except to make us miserable, broke and physically sick. They hold us back because they are monuments to our disappointment and shame. However, the cross and resurrection of Jesus Christ can obliterate them. Second, we must get out of the tombstone building business. Whatever happens, let it go! Whether it is sickness, financial setback, disappointment, divorce or any other thing – for the sake of your own spiritual health and well-being, refuse to build a monument in your soul.

You can use the following decrees to overcome trauma and tear down the tombstones in your life.

I repent for allowing a painful traumatic event or circumstance to become a tombstone in my soul. I forgive anyone who wounded me and caused one of these tombs to be erected in my inner man. I put the blood of Jesus on every area of my soul where I have set up these memorials and markers and I tear them down by the power of the cross and through resurrection, dunamis power. Jesus came out of His tomb through resurrection power. I release resurrection power into my tombs so that the stone can roll away and I can be free! (Matthew 6:12-15, 1 John 1:7, Philippians 3:10)

I decree every monument and memorial in my mind, will and emotions is being erased by the power of the blood and dunamis power. All the painful thoughts connected to that traumatic event that keep haunting my mind are being removed right now. Every tombstone that controls my will and causes me to make bad decisions is being healed by the cross and the resurrection. Every old dead memory that lives in my emotions is being healed. I will not be depressed anxious, worried or fearful anymore because I do not dwell among the tombs. (Ephesians 1:7, Hebrews 9:14, 22 and 10:19, 22)

I decree the law of the Spirit of life in Christ has freed my soul from the law of sin and of death. *"For God has done what the Law could not do …"*. He sent *"His own Son in the guise of sinful flesh and as an offering for sin, [God] condemned sin in the flesh, [subdued, overcame, deprived it of its power] over me"* (Romans 8:2-4).

I decree I am a new creation in Jesus Christ. As His love, His blood and His power have filled my soul; the former things have passed away. All the bad memories that formed tombs in my soul are being removed right now by the blood and power of Jesus Christ. Forgetting what lies behind and straining forward to what lies ahead, I press on toward the goal to win the prize to which God in Christ Jesus is calling us upward. (2 Corinthians 5:17, Philippians 3:13-14)

I decree my soul will bless the Lord who has forgiven all my iniquities, healed all of my diseases and redeemed my life from the pit and corruption. He crowned me with loving-kindness and tender mercy. (Psalm 103:3-4)

I decree the Lord has forgiven my sins and healed my inner self. He will protect me and keep me alive; He will cause me to be called blessed in the land. The Lord will sustain, refresh, *and* strengthen me and deliver me in the time of trouble and trauma. (Psalm 41:2-4, Psalm 50:15)

I decree the Sun of Righteousness is rising with healing in His wings *and* His beams on every area of my soul that has a tomb in it. His glory and His light will heal those painful memories and cause me to be transformed into His image from glory to glory. Because I am healed of all trauma I will *"go forth and gambol like a calf [released] from the stall and leap for joy."* (Malachi 4:2) (2 Corinthians 3:18)

The woman with the issue of blood was traumatized by her 12-year-long sickness. She spent all the money she had, suffered under the hands of her physicians and grew no better, but worse. But she was healed of all trauma she endured when she touched the wings of Christ's prayer shawl and her soul took refuge under the shadow of His wings. Jesus said He felt dunamis leave Him and she became excellent of soul. **I decree** the same for me. I have suffered for many years from trauma but I believe the dunamis power that is in my spirit is being released into my soul and body to heal me now. I forgive anyone who made me suffer like those physicians made the woman with the issue of blood suffer, and I repent of being angry with them. I receive the blood of Jesus into my soul and I release dunamis power from my spirit into my inner man so I can be excellent of soul. I am being healed as my soul takes refuge under the shadow of His wings. (Luke 8:43-48, Ephesians 3:16, Psalm 57:1)

CHAPTER TEN

DECREES TO DEFEAT THE KINGDOM OF DARKNESS

Perhaps you know how King David felt when he wrote these words: *"For the enemy has pursued and persecuted my soul, he has crushed my life down to the ground; he has made me to dwell in dark places as those who have long been dead"* (Psalm 143:3).

Satan and his demons are constantly looking for a way to get a foothold in your life. When the devil sees a wounded soul, he is delighted, because he knows he has a legal right to torment you and establish a beachhead for his forces. But the blood and dunamis power will enable you to crush the forces of darkness and be declared "off limits" to Satan and his minions.

Here's proof of what I'm saying. In John 14:30, Jesus says, *"I will not talk with you much more, for the prince, (evil genius, ruler) of the world is coming. And he has no claim on Me. [He has nothing in common with Me; there is nothing in Me that belongs to him, so he has no power over Me.]"*

One of the reasons that Jesus, as a man, had complete dominion over the enemy was that He had nothing in His soul, or spirit, that was in common with the demonic.

When Jesus cast out Legion, in Mark 5:7, the demon asked Him, *"What have You to do with me, Jesus, Son of the Most High God? [What is there in common between us?] I solemnly implore You by God, do not begin to torment me!"*

Legion recognized there was something different about Jesus. Legion knew that Jesus had nothing in Him that was in common with that foul spirit. That huge demonic spirit could find no common ground in Jesus' soul that would give him the legal right to torment Jesus. As you get healed in your soul, you will have nothing in common with the enemy, so he will have no power over any part of your life!

Make these decrees so that you can be healed of everything you have in common with the adversary of your soul!

I decree I have been forgiven and declared righteous through the blood of Jesus and made whole through the power of His resurrection. I am a new creation in Christ and my sins have been cast into the furthest depths of the sea. Every sin that I have in common with Satan is being washed by the blood. Every wound in my soul that I have in common with him is being filled with the dunamis power that lives in my spirit. Therefore, I refuse to listen to Satan when he accuses me or causes me to remember my past sins and failures. He is a liar and the father of lies. I am not under condemnation because I belong to Jesus Christ. (2 Corinthians 5:17, Romans 3:25 and 8:1)

I decree Jesus Christ is washing my soul in His blood and disarming the evil powers and authorities that are over me right now. He is triumphing over them and making a public spectacle of them at the cross, according to Colossians 2:15.

I decree I have nothing in common with Satan or His demons because of the blood of Jesus and His dunamis power. Through faith in Christ, I am a child of the King, and impervious to attacks of the devil. I am living daily in God's promise that *"You will not fear the terror of night, nor the arrow that flies by day, nor the pestilence that stalks in the darkness, nor the plague that destroys at midday. A thousand may fall at your side, ten thousand at your right hand, but it will not come near you."* (Psalm 91:5-7, NIV)

I decree just like the woman that was bent over by a spirit of infirmity, I am being loosed from the power of Satan to keep me bound. The word infirmity means weakness and infirmity of the body and soul. I loose the power of the blood and dunamis into every area in my body and soul that is infirmed. I decree that I am infirmed no more and every spirit of infirmity has to go now in Jesus' name. (Luke 13:11-16)

I decree my life and soul are hidden in Jesus Christ, and that the devil does not have the power to oppress, harass or attack me. Jesus defeated the enemy with dunamis power. Acts 10:38 says God anointed Jesus Christ with the Holy Spirit and power (dunamis) and he healed everyone who was oppressed by the devil. I decree to the enemy that I have the same power living in me that Jesus used to heal people of the devils assaults!

I decree both my body and my soul are clothed with the full armor of God, which makes me able to stand my ground against the forces of evil and extinguish all the flaming arrows of the evil one. (Ephesians 6:11-18)

I decree because I am filled with the Spirit and dunamis power of God, greater is He that is in me than He that is in the world. Satan has no claim over me. God has given me the power to drive out demons in the name of Jesus Christ. (1 John 4:4, Mark 16:17)

I decree Jesus Christ has given me full access to the cleansing power of His blood and He has filled me with His dunamis power. Now I have full authority to trample on snakes and scorpions and to overcome all the power of my enemy, the devil. Nothing will harm me, and I rejoice that my name is written in heaven. (Luke 10:18-20)

I decree I have been set free from all weaknesses and infirmities caused by the devil and his demons. My soul and body have been filled with dunamis, light and glory, and I no longer live in bondage. I am like the woman bound by a demon of sickness for eighteen years. She was bent completely forward and utterly unable to straighten herself up *or* to look upward, but she was set free in an instant by the power and presence of Jesus. (Luke 13:11-13)

AFTERWORD

Now that you have read the book, I hope you agree with my opening statement, "It is small but mighty."

If you know my story, you know that I spent most of my life learning lessons the hard way. I repeated the same mistakes early and often, expecting better results every time, the classic definition of insanity, they say.

After one of my "adventures" went painfully wrong, landing me in federal prison, I faced a long sentence and a major decision. My way was clearly not working. Was there a better way? The answer came in a book I had never read and, up until that point, had never even been a curiosity for me. But, I had plenty of time, and I had a King James Bible. As I read this ancient tome, I found my life revealed, page by page. It is impossible for me to describe the way that book immediately and forever gripped my heart. I accepted Jesus and my life spun 180 degrees at that very moment. I went from hurting people to hurting *for* them. I needed desperately to make a difference for God.

The revelations you just read, and the decrees that emanated from them, are the result of untold hours of research and time spent in the presence of God's Holy Spirit. During those hours, days and weeks, I felt a compelling drive to learn why, though I tried so hard to live righteously, I still suffered in my body, my relationships, my finances and my emotions. Most of the sincere, God-fearing people around me seemed caught in the same cycle. "Why, God?" I cried. "We are your children. We are royalty and joint heirs with Christ! Why are we living beneath your promises? Why do we seek You but so seldom find You?!"

And God, in His infinite wisdom and patience, began to impart to me scripture upon scripture, precept upon precept. "Jesus saves and perfects the spirit immediately, but the soul ... the soul ... that custodian of every experience good and bad throughout the generations. ... the soul takes longer."

I challenge you to use this little book as a reference tool. Depending on what is happening in your life, some chapters may resonate stronger than others. Bookmark those pages that speak to you and state those decrees every day. You will begin to see a positive difference in your life. And, please don't despair if it does not happen overnight. It has taken a very long time to get where you are today, so keep working on your soul and rejoice in every victory.

God has done amazing miracles in my life and He, being no respecter of persons, will do the same for you. I am confident of that.

In the Father's love,

Kate

END NOTES

Foreword

[1] p.12, (Dictionary and Word Search for "live")
(Strong's G2198), Strong's Concordance, Blue Letter Bible. https://www.blueletterbible.org/lang/Lexicon/Lexicon.cfm?strongs=G2198&t=KJV

[2] p.13 (Dictionary and Word Search for "save")
(Strong's G4982), Strong's Concordance, Blue Letter Bible. https://www.blueletterbible.org/lang/Lexicon/Lexicon.cfm?strongs=G4982&t=KJV

Chapter One: The Wounded Soul

[3] p.20 (Dictionary and Word Search for "infirmity")
(Strong's G769). Strong's Concordance, Blue Letter Bible. (https://www.blueletterbible.org/lang/Lexicon/Lexicon.cfm?strongs=G769&t=KJV

Chapter Two: Two Simple Remedies for Your Soul

[4] p. 27,29,37 (Dictionary and Word Search for "power")
(Strong's G1411). Strong's Concordance, Blue Letter Bible. https://www.blueletterbible.org/lang/Lexicon/Lexicon.cfm?strongs=G1411&t=KJV

[5] p.30 (Dictionary and Word Search for "inner'")
(Strong's G2080), Strong's Concordance, Blue Letter Bible. https://www.blueletterbible.org/lang/Lexicon/Lexicon.cfm?strongs=G2080&t=KJV

Chapter Three: The Glory and the Light

[6] p.36 (Dictionary and Word Search for "glory")
(Strong's GH3513), Strong's Concordance, Blue Letter Bible.
https://www.blueletterbible.org/lang/Lexicon/Lexicon.cfm?strongs=H3513&t=KJV

[7] p.38 (Dictionary and Word Search for "glory")
"(Strong's G1391).S trong's Concordance, Blue Letter Bible.

https://www.blueletterbible.org/lang/lexicon/lexicon.
cfm?strongs=G1391

[8] p.39 (Dictionary and Word Search for "healing")
(Strong's G3513). Strong's Concordance, Blue Letter Bible.
https://www.blueletterbible.org/lang/Lexicon/Lexicon.
cfm?strongs=H4832&t=KJV

[9] p. 39,72 (Dictionary and Word Search for "dark")
(Strong's G4655). Strong's Concordance, Blue Letter Bible.
https://www.blueletterbible.org/lang/Lexicon/lexicon.
cfm?strongs=G4655&t=KJV

[10] p. 42 (Dictionary and Word Search for "praise")
(Strong's H3313). Strong's Concordance, Blue Letter Bible. https://www.
blueletterbible.org/lang/lexicon/lexicon.cfm?Strongs=H3313&t=KJV

Chapter 4: Grace

[11] p. 43,69 (Dictionary and Word Search for "grace")
(Strong's G5485). Strong's Concordance, Blue Letter Bible.
https://www.blueletterbible.org/lang/Lexicon/Lexicon.
cfm?strongs=G5485&t=KJV

[12] p. 49 (Dictionary and Word Search for "full")
(Strong's G4134).Strong's Concordance, Blue Letter Bible.
https://www.blueletterbible.org/lang/Lexicon/Lexicon.
cfm?strongs=G4134&t=KJV